Aspen explode into fall gold, Utah.
LARRY ULRICH

Sunset over the Sawtooth Mountains, Idaho.
JEFF GNASS

Exploring the
NORTHERN
ROCKIES

A Companion Press Book

by Kathy Tyers

In memory of
William McQueen Freeburg
1925–1990

Produced and edited by Jane Freeburg
Designed by Linda Trujillo

Printed and bound in Korea through Bolton Associates,
San Rafael, California
ISBN 0-944197-13-2

CONTENTS

Opposite: Fallen leaves, Colorado.
JC LEACOCK

From top: Historic business in Virginia City, Montana.
SANDY NYKERK

A double rainbow leads to adventure along a Montana highway.
JOHN TYERS

Cross country skiing in Grand Tetons National Park, Wyoming.
TOM BEAN

A herd of horses in the Gallatin National Forest, Montana.
DAN TYERS

Across the Great Divide

Exploring the northern Rocky Mountains of the United States, the traveler treks up and down a continent's forested backbone, crossing rivers and streams that feed three distant oceans. From central Colorado to the Canadian border, this system of imposing mountain ranges dramatizes events reaching back to the dawn of geological time.

About 65 million years ago, planetary stresses began to push the Pacific Plate of the Earth's crust against its North American Plate neighbor (rock *will* fold, under enough force and over enough time). The Pacific Plate dropped beneath the North American Plate, pressing it up to raise the Rocky Mountain chain. Blocks of the North American Plate faulted—snapped under stress—and broke loose, continuing to rise, drop, and slide against one another for thirty million years. Varying rock types were upthrust and warped by these forces, creating contours of several distinct characters. At the south end of this region, the Front Range at Rocky Mountain National Park is a broad upland of primarily igneous rock. The slow steady force of river erosion gouged out canyons along the edges of the southern Rockies, cutting through millions of years of sea-bottom sedimentary deposits to stone as ancient as the continent. In many areas cracked and faulted by continental stress, superheated magma forced its way up through sedimentary layers, solidifying below the surface into igneous formations that were later exposed by uplift and erosion.

Contrasting with the Front Range, the Lewis Range of Waterton-Glacier International Peace Park at the Canadian border exposes layers of softer sedimentary limestone, siltstone, and argillites. Glaciers born of a global cooling trend roughly two million years ago scoured into

Above: Blue columbine and lichen, Medicine Bow National Forest, Wyoming.
LARRY ULRICH

Opposite: The Grand Tetons reflected in still waters of a beaver pond.
DENNIS FLAHERTY

Top: Clouds over the Teton Range, Wyoming.
CHUCK PLACE

shallow valleys that had already been slowly excavated by water flow. Swifter than water erosion, these rivers of ice dug classic U-shaped valleys with tall, sheer sides. The glaciers left piles of stone and debris, chains of rock-basin lakes, and magnificent cirques—shallow mountainside bowls that often contain lakes draining in spectacular waterfalls.

In both regions, newly uplifted mountain ranges forced moisture-laden clouds blowing in from the Pacific Ocean to rise and cross from the west. In higher, cooler layers of the atmosphere, clouds drop their moisture as snow or rain. This weather pattern has made erosion—by water or ice, depending upon world climate—a major force in shaping the Rockies.

Up until the time of the Rockies' creation, dinosaurs and their kin had roamed the margins of a vast inland sea. Buried where they lived, the remains of many lay fossilized deep in the sediment, later to be revealed by those mountain-building forces—uplift and erosion. At Utah's Dinosaur National Monument and Wyoming's Fossil Butte National Monument, the fossils can be viewed in place, while the Museum of the Rockies boasts a collection of fossils unearthed all over Montana. Metal ores are found in the Rockies, too. Where liquified quartz laden with mineral ions rose to the top of hot magma, it crept into rock cracks, creating deposits rich in precious metals.

A dizzying variety of plant and animal species now lives along the Rocky Mountains. Their biological niches overlap, influenced by elevation and northward latitude. Some regions butt up against stony desert and support cacti, lizards, and small rodents that are hunted by the fox and coyote. In other areas, foothills abound with plant life watered by snowmelt and streams. More and larger animals, such as deer and badgers, share these more vegetated regions with a variety of birds. High on the mountain slopes, sub-alpine ecosystems are habitat for species such as elk and bear. They give way to krummholz—dwarf forest—and above the treeline, to tundra, the domain of whistling marmots and tiny, haymaking pika.

As the seasons change, wildlife moves up and down the mountainsides. Summer's solitude and rich, abundant forage draw bighorn and elk up into higher meadows. Predators and scavengers follow: the ubiquitous coyote, the northerly wolf, and the rarely observed bobcat and mountain lion that still stalk their ancestral prey high in Rocky Mountain forests and parks.

Inhabited by Native American tribes for centuries before the thirteen New England colonies became the United States of America, the Rockies provided game, building materials, and sacred grounds for many western tribes. These included the Arapaho, Bannock, Blackfeet,

Opposite: The backbone of a continent, the Continental Divide as experienced from Glacier National Park's Swiftcurrent Lookout, Montana
RICK JACKSON

Above: Rock formations characteristic of the Colorado Plateau frame Green River, Dinosaur National Monument, Colorado.
JEFF GNASS

Left: Bull elk grazing at sunrise, Yellowstone National Park, Wyoming.
GLENN VAN NIMWEGEN

Crow, Flathead, Fremont, Gros Ventre, Hopi, Kiowa, Nez Perce, Northern Cheyenne, Sheepeater, Shoshone, Sioux, and Ute. Countless place names in the Rocky Mountain west remain as their legacy. Inch by inch, the tribes gave ground to Pacific-bound pioneers, although Custer Battlefield National Monument in southern Montana marks the site of one Indian victory. Yet the invasion of "modern" lifestyle proceeds inexorably, permeating reservations as two cultures struggle for equilibrium. How much of Earth's native culture could we preserve if our world were invaded by technologically superior aliens?

Meriwether Lewis and William Clark, sent by President Thomas Jefferson to survey the Louisiana Purchase, crossed the continental divide—a line separating the Atlantic and Pacific

Above: Brilliant colors at Grand Prismatic Spring, Yellowstone National Park.
SANDY NYKERK

Opposite, top: Jagged skyline of the Beartooth Mountains, Montana.
TOM NELSON

Below, right: A mountain lion and her cub.
LEWIS KEMPER

Ocean watersheds—in Montana in 1805, but the area was not settled until much later. An imposing obstacle to wagon travel, the Rockies blocked easy westward movement to rich, temperate Pacific coastlands. Yet wildlife—and the European craze for beaver-felt hats—drew in trappers and fur traders (only the beaver's short underfur was used to make beaver felt, and the hides went to glue makers). When mountain men such as John Colter and Jim Bridger relayed tales of mountain splendor back to "civilization" in the east or on the west coast, educated listeners often scoffed.

Still, in the second half of the 1800s, precious metals did bring the white man and his accomplices—Asian immigrants and recently liberated slaves. Explorers followed ancient Indian trail systems to breach the Rockies. Those trails often led along rivers, which provided a critical water supply and approached the mountains' lowest passes. Through South Pass, a mesquite saddle in southern Wyoming, ran the Big Medicine Trail. Opened to wagon traffic in the 1840s, Big Medicine became the historic Oregon Trail. The only other major route westward crossed the continental divide far south in New Mexico.

Ranching followed mining, and so did the timber industry that still supplies urban areas nationwide. Most recently have come the vacationers. Improved rail and air service, and highways—which run, like the trails, where the mountains and rivers dictate they must—make mid-continental grandeur easier and safer to reach and to enjoy.

Left: Grizzly bear.
DIANA STRATTON

Above: A yellow-bellied marmot basking in the sun.
GLENN VAN NIMWEGEN

Mountain Fastness

CHAPTER TWO

Lazy, cool mornings when elk and deer come down to browse, warm afternoons full of brilliant sunshine, and chilly mountain nights watched by a million brittle stars present a picture of Colorado summertime. In winter, Rocky Mountain parks and resorts draw vacationers anxious to savor the snow, the crisp cold air, and deep quiet.

Rocky Mountain National Park

Crystalline igneous rock—granite and related stone types—creates the spectacular skyline of this alpine National Park. Small living glaciers survive at higher elevations, while the work of larger ancient glaciers dominates the mountain scenery.

To the Arapaho Indians, Longs Peak and Mount Meeker were *nesotaieux*—the Two Guides—visible for miles around. Low on the Park's sunny slopes grow ponderosa pine and juniper, and on hillsides facing north there is Douglas fir. As altitude rises, groundcover changes. Above 9,000 feet grow Englemann spruce and subalpine fir. Krummholz, stunted "elfin timber," dominates the upper edges of the zone below treeline.

Fully a third of Rocky Mountain National Park lies above treeline, and a quarter of the plant species growing in alpine areas can also be found in the Arctic. To survive in the tundra, where the growing season is often as short as ten weeks, plants remain small, with short stems and few branches. Five-year-old plants sometimes are smaller than the end of a finger. Small leaves secrete waxy coatings, or grow thick and succulent to conserve moisture. Some develop hairy surfaces to lessen abrasion from ice and dirt.

Above: Bear Lake, Rocky Mountain National Park.
JEFF GNASS

Opposite: The Maroon Bells, near Aspen, Colorado.
JC LEACOCK

Top: Aspen and spruce in fall.
LARRY ULRICH

Above: Clouds hover below 14,255-foot Longs Peak.
TOM TILL

Right: Trail Ridge Road traverses Rocky Mountain National Park's alpine tundra, with open vistas of Longs Peak.
JEFF GNASS

Treeline itself varies. Between eleven and twelve thousand feet, a few gnarled trees survive in spots protected from drying winds where there is sufficient sunlight. Weather conditions are so critical that one boulder's shelter or a winter covering of snow can mean survival. A waist-high tree may be hundreds of years old, each inch of trunk diameter representing a century's slow growth.

Traversed early in the nineteenth century by French fur traders, the Rockies' Front Range west of the Denver area was a major obstacle to nineteenth-century emigrants traveling west. Unwilling to cross such a barrier with their families, wagons, and animals, settlers avoided the Rockies' steepest slopes by turning north across Wyoming or south along the Santa Fe trail through New Mexico.

In 1859, Joel Estes and his son rode into what is now called the Estes Valley. Travel writer Isabella Bird passed through the Front Range in 1873 on her way to England from the Sandwich Islands (Hawaii). Mostly riding horseback with a rough mountain guide, she ascended Longs Peak in a long skirt and boots. Inspired by the view, she wrote in *A Lady's Life in the Rocky Mountains*, originally published in 1879, "Nature, rioting in her grandest mood, exclaimed with voices of grandeur, solitude, sublimity, beauty, and infinity, 'Lord, what is man, that Thou art mindful of him?'"

The ranching town of Estes Park grew up at the eastern edge of contemporary Rocky Mountain National Park, which was established by Congress in 1915. Now Estes Park supports a booming tourism industry.

Crossing Rocky Mountain National Park from east to west, Trail Ridge Road reaches a maximum 12,183 feet in elevation. Almost 3 miles of this highway lie above 12,000 feet, in thin air that makes automotive vapor lock common and foot travel a challenge. The drive must be taken slowly, but rewarding vistas stretch out on every side. This treeless world, so like Arctic tundra . . . brilliant colors, glacial landscapes, and abundant wildlife . . . makes the fifty-mile trip a spiritual and emotional pilgrimage.

The unpaved 1920s-era road across this parkland had hairpin curves so tight that to get around them, motorists had to back up several times toward dangerous slopes. Parts of that original road climbed 16% grades. The present Trail Ridge Road follows a different route and utilizes carefully engineered grades. First opened in 1932, it is named for an ancient, stone-marked Ute Indian trail across the high country, which the present road crosses half a dozen times.

Above, left: Columbine, Colorado's state flower, bursts from rocky crevices.
JC LEACOCK

Above: Patrol cabin at Thunder Lake, Rocky Mountain National Park.
LARRY ULRICH

Left: Rocky mountain mule deer.
PAUL R JOHNSON

Climbers and hikers can enjoy Rocky Mountain National Park on an intimate, personal level. More than 350 miles of trails carry hikers into back country where elk and deer browse among a myriad of wildflowers. 14,255-foot Longs Peak is a popular climb, but it's advisable to start early in order to reach the summit by noon and be off before afternoon lightning storms may make the peak's vicinity treacherous.

For backcountry visitors with special physical needs, Rocky Mountain National Park provides Handicamp. A backcountry camping area specifically designed for the disabled, Handicamp is maintained by the Park Service and available year round on a free permit basis—as are over 200 other backcountry campsites in the park.

Above: Double rainbow over Crested Butte.
DENNIS FLAHERTY

Right: Main Street, Leadville, Colorado.
JC LEACOCK

Far Right: Musicians entertain skiers—Bavarian style—at Colorado's Beaver Creek Resort.
FRED GEBHART

Colorado Mountain Resorts

Aspen, Breckenridge, Copper Mountain, Keystone, Powderhorn, Purgatory, and Vail: The names fall like incantations from the lips of western skiers. These developed districts on the Rockies' slopes also appeal to the summer visitor: Knee-high with flowers or chest-deep in powder snow, Colorado's mountain resorts inspire travelers to return many times. Victorian architecture, museums, and shopping opportunities satisfy the less adventurous, with festivals for music and the visual arts held annually at several locations.

Leadville

Uplift and erosion reveal quartz veins rich in metal ore at several locations up and down the Rockies. The first documented strike in the Leadville sector was in April 1860, when Alan Lee washed the first placer gold in what became the California mining district. After Lee's find, Leadville boomed. Gold, silver, lead . . . virtually every desirable metal was extracted. Nearby Oro City mines produced ten tons of gold in less than a decade. By 1880 the booming area's population broke 30,000. Again in the 1940s, Leadville prospered: World War Two created a strong market for molybdenum, a metal that hardens steel.

Located at the edge of Pike National Forest, Leadville's museums and narrow-gauge railroad preserve the area's colorful mining history. Trails attract mountain bikers from all over the region. Numerous rousing summer-stock theaters entertain the town's guests.

Black Canyon of the Gunnison National Monument

The Gunnison River established its course over soft volcanic rock about two million years ago. Once through the easily eroded layer, the river began to carve older crystalline layers of schist and gneiss. The resultant nearly vertical chasm penetrates to a maximum depth of 2,700 feet, and from ledge to ledge The Narrows stand only 1,300 feet wide. Dim sunlight shines on dark stone inside the Black Canyon of the Gunnison only a few hours a day.

Archeological evidence suggests that prehistoric man, and later the Ute Indians, used only the canyon rims and never lived in the gorge. By the end of the 1800s, settlers hoped to tap the Gunnison River to supply water for the Uncompahgre Valley. In 1900, five area men tried to float through the canyon with surveying equipment, but after a month's effort, they turned back. Later explorers, using a rubber mattress for a raft, finally surveyed the Black Canyon in 1901. And in 1909, a six-mile irrigation tunnel opened to carry water from a point just outside National Monument boundaries to thirsty local farming communities.

Many spots along its north and south rim roads (which do not connect within Park boundaries) overlook the Black Canyon. Below one South Rim vantage is the Painted Wall, where pressure from below forced molten material into cracks and joints of the base rock, creating an effect that resembles overly marbled beef. Peregrine falcons nest on the wall, freely riding its updrafts inside one of Colorado's last shelter spots for this endangered species.

Colorado National Monument

A semi-desert on the northeastern edge of the Colorado Plateau, Colorado National Monument is a mile-high province of horizontal sedimentary rock cut by deep canyons. Coyotes and canyon wrens share the plateau with falcons, ravens, desert bighorns, and an occasional mountain lion.

A huge area adjacent to the Rockies, the Colorado Plateau actually consists of several plateaus. This one, the Uncompahgre, was named by Ute Indians to signify "place where water makes red rock." Like the nearby Rockies, the Uncompahgre is part of an ancient uplift.

Erosion in Colorado National Monument exposes sandstones, shales, and other sedimentary rocks, some more resistant than others to wind-borne sand grains and the digging force of water. One particularly hard layer, the Kayenta Formation, lies like a protective cap over Independence Monument and other dramatic rock forms. Other more rounded formations attest to the Kayenta's eventual weathering away, allowing accelerated erosion of softer stone beneath.

Above: The deep gorge at Black Canyon of the Gunnison National Monument.
JOHN VAVRUSKA

Left: A coyote hunts for his breakfast.
DIANA STRATTON

Below: Golden eagle.
DIANA STRATTON

17

One reliable way to judge elevation in these plateau lands is to look at the foliage. Below 6,000 feet, Utah junipers dominate. From 6,000 up to 8,500 is the realm of the pinon pine—short-needled evergreens with rich, sweet seeds that were a vital food source for Native Americans and explorers.

Ute Indians once occupied half of Utah and two-thirds of Colorado, including this area. After summering high in the game-filled mountains, families descended to warmer valleys for winter encampments.

One man, John Otto, deserves much of the credit for the setting aside of this National Monument. Thought by many local folks to be crazy, Otto lived alone in the desolate canyons southwest of Grand Junction, Colorado. From there he campaigned, raised funds, and wrote letters encouraging the government to set aside this area for future generations' enjoyment. He built miles of trails to allow others to see its wonders. When President William H. Taft established Colorado National Monument in 1911, John Otto became its first caretaker . . . for just one dollar a month.

Rim Rock Drive climbs from the Grand Valley of the Colorado River to the edge of the high plateau, then winds along its edge. Ideal for bicycling as well as auto and motorcycling tours, the breathtaking 23-mile drive is open for travel virtually 365 days a year.

The Colorado River flows through nearby Grand Junction on its way from headwaters in Rocky Mountain National Park to its mighty Grand Canyon. Travelers along Interstate 70 parallel the wide, muddy Colorado for a number of miles between Grand Junction and the high Rockies.

About ten miles west of Colorado National Monument, another unique route leaves Inter-

state 70. Kokopelli's Trail, named for the humpbacked flute player of Native American legend, was constructed by hundreds of volunteers and stretches 128 miles from Loma Boat Launch near Grand Junction through desert canyons to Moab, Utah. Kokopelli's Trail is a combination of county roads, sand and dirt lanes, and single-track trails. Designed for mountain bike use, the route also accommodates hikers and—along some sections—four-wheeled vehicles. No drinking water is available along the trail.

Above: Bluebells, indian paintbrush, and lupine color a lush hillside in Colorado's Snowmass Wilderness.
JC LEACOCK

Left: An alpine waterfall.
JC LEACOCK

Beginnings of Time

ot all of the Rocky Mountain country reaches for treeline. In Utah, Idaho, and southern Wyoming, ancient waterways provide a glimpse at the distant past. Lava flowed here, too; and mountainous spurs—which originated in the same uplift and overthrust period as the Rockies—thread several paths through the northeastern corner of Utah.

Dinosaur National Monument

On this quarry site roughly 150 million years ago, at a sandbar near the inside of a river bend—or so paleontologists envision it—dinosaur carcasses washed ashore, were scavenged by carnivores, and later buried and fossilized.

The age of the dinosaurs ended almost simultaneously (from the long-eyed view of geologists) with the Laramide Orogeny, the mountain-building period that created the Rocky Mountains 65 million years ago. In the Dinosaur National Monument area, rock strata of the Colorado Plateau folded and faulted to become part of the Rocky Mountain complex.

An astonishing variety of plants and animals live at Dinosaur National Monument. Several fish species occupy unique ecological niches in the sediment-laden, summer-warm waters of the Green and Yampa rivers. Some local soils contain the toxic element selenium, but several species of desert plants have developed the ability to absorb selenium without harm, and they now live only on those otherwise poisonous soil types.

Human habitation of the Dinosaur National Monument area has always centered around water. Deep canyons at the confluence of Dinosaur's two rivers make "linear oases" along its desert floor. In these places, early inhabitants of the region—Paleoindians, Archaic, Fremont, and

Above: Fossil fish, Fossil Butte National Monument, Wyoming.
PAT & BOB MOMICH

Opposite: The sinuous Yampa River from Harding Hole Overlook, Dinosaur National Monument.
CRAIG LINDSAY

Top: Sunrise over Split Mountain, Dinosaur National Monument.
JEFF GNASS

Most of Dinosaur National Monument extends along the Green and Yampa rivers in Colorado, but its Visitor Center is accessed from Utah Highway 149. The Visitor Center stands partly upon the ledge where the first fossils were found, and it protects a rock face where more than 2,000 fossil bones lie *in situ* (as originally found) at various states of excavation. Other informational exhibits make fascinating browsing.

In Dinosaur's rugged back country, white-water rafters can pit their skills against stretches of river that inspired explorers to christen them with names such as Disaster Falls and Hell's Half Mile.

Bridgerland and Logan

Utahns call the northeast corner of their state "Bridgerland" after the famous mountain man and scout, Jim Bridger, who is credited as the first white man to set eyes on the Great Salt Lake in 1824. European demand for beaver-felt hats instigated the brief but colorful and romantic period of Western history known as the Mountain Man era. At the peak of the Rocky Mountain fur trade, this quarter lay at a major crossroad for traders. Rendezvous—annual gatherings of the mountain men—were held in Bridgerland in 1826 and 1827. These were wild affairs, when everything available in the West changed hands. When European males began to favor silk hats instead of beaver, trade collapsed; but mountain men opened the Indian trails that were later used by emigrants.

Deep in Bridgerland lies Logan Canyon, where a U.S. Forest Service National Scenic Byway leads past towering cliffs, rugged rockfalls, and fossil sites, with many improved campgrounds and picnic spots along the way.

Logan Valley was named after Ephraim Logan, a fur trapper. The nearby city of Logan, home of Utah State University, boasts numerous historic buildings—each a testament to pioneer tenacity. Among other programs, the University conducts cutting-edge space technology research. Bridgerland is a winter mecca for snowmobilers and cross-country skiers, and alpine skiers enjoy uncrowded Beaver Mountain Resort.

Cache National Forest

High above Cache Valley tower the Wasatch Mountains, and autumn reds and golds make the Cache National Forest shimmer. The Cache Valley was a favorite place for trappers to "cache" or conceal their furs and supplies until needed for trading or consumption. In some places, holes in the earth show where nineteenth-century trappers stashed up to a ton—sometimes more—of pelts and other property.

Nearby Bear Lake's brook, rainbow, and native cutthroat trout keep anglers casting, and sailboating is popular along Bear Lake's forested shores.

Above: A paleontologist studies fossilized dinosaur bones, Dinosaur National Monument.
JEFF GNASS

Right: Fremont culture petroglyphs at McKee Springs, Dinosaur National Monument.
JEFF GNASS

later the Ute tribes—hunted game. On cliff faces and canyon walls naturally darkened by "desert varnish" (a deposit of mineral oxides or organic matter), Fremont artists chipped or scratched through to a lighter colored sandstone. Pictographs of animals, human figures, and geometric abstracts have survived for more than a millennium etched into the patinas of weathered desert rock.

Dinosaur National Monument was established in 1915 and enlarged in 1938 to include nearly 100 miles of the Green and Yampa Rivers. In the 1950s, proposed dam building inside the Monument's boundaries created a national test case: Would lands designated as National Parks or National Monuments remain undeveloped, or could they be reopened for commercial exploitation? Debate raged in Congress, accompanied by a national outcry. Grudgingly, the dams' proponents backed off. The Echo Park Dam Project was never built.

*Aspen cover the
shoulders of Mt.
Timpaganos, Uinta
National Forest,
Utah.*
LARRY ULRICH

23

Wyoming

Ranked ninth in size among U.S. states yet a distant fiftieth in population, Wyoming boasts a sparse population density of only five people per square mile. Its wilderness survives comparatively unchanged. Just south of the cowboy state's southwestern corner, the Uinta Mountains jut eastward out of the Wasatch Range. Nestled north of the Uintas inside this angle lie two of Wyoming's less-traveled attractions.

Flaming Gorge National Recreation Area

Flaming Gorge Reservoir links the mountainous environment of northern Utah—where much of the reservoir lies inside brilliant redrock vertical canyon walls—with the broad shale deserts of southern Wyoming. Nearby petroglyphs (carvings and inscriptions on stone) and Indian artifacts remind visitors that Native Americans lived and hunted in this region for centuries. The deep red gorges of the Utah portion are considered Flaming Gorge Reservoir's most scenic areas, but the northerly stretches of water surrounded by desert have visual drama of their own.

Circled by a loop road accessible from Interstate 80, Flaming Gorge Reservoir is called by locals "the fishing hot spot of America" and offers trout fishing all year round. Other lake activities include camping, boating, and water skiing. Along the shores lie prime photographic opportunities, such as the play of light and shadow on living-color rock formations, or desert and mountain wildlife in diverse habitats.

Fossil Butte National Monument

Roughly 120 miles northwest of Dinosaur National Monument, near Kemmerer in southwestern Wyoming, another slice of fossil history lies sandwiched atop brightly colored beds of the Wasatch formation and below Fossil Butte's pale weathered summit. An ancient lake lapped at its shores here some fifty million years ago. Fish by the thousands died and settled undisturbed to a mucky bottom, where they were rapidly buried by blankets of sediment that gradually turned to hard rock. Whole skeletons have been preserved, some with delicate fins, tail rays, and even their scales intact. Found at Fossil Butte are the remains of perch, herring, paddlefish, gar, and stingray, as well as animals, insects, and many kinds of plants.

The meat of this fossil sandwich, where most of Fossil Butte's specimens for more than 100 years have been found, is a section of laminated limestone averaging only 18 inches thick. Other layers of the butte contain fossils, but not in such concentration.

Fossil Butte's Visitor Center provides hiking information and a series of exhibits. An interpretive trail near the Center leads to old fossil quarries.

Above: Late afternoon at Fossil Butte National Monument, Wyoming.
JEFF GNASS

Right: Pronghorn antelope buck.
GLENN VAN NIMWEGEN

Idaho

After passing landmarks Independence Rock and Split Rock in Wyoming, pioneers on the Oregon Trail crossed South Pass (now on U.S. Highway 287) and proceeded westward across southern Idaho. Wagon ruts worn into rugged sandstone terrain still mark their route in several places, deep scars that will probably outlast contemporary highways. During peak years between 1849 and 1853, the Oregon Trail at times looked like a solid line of white canvas-topped prairie schooners slowly sailing west across low hills and dusty deserts. Much of the schooner captains' wilderness now lies green with Idahoan agriculture.

Craters of the Moon National Monument

Lava flows and cinder cones, remnants of volcanic activity along the Great Rift, make up the landscape of Craters of the Moon National Monument. Southwest of Arco along Idaho Highway 20, cracks, craters, and spatter cones show where molten lava spewed from the ground as recently as 2,100 years ago. Some lava tubes, once filled with liquid rock, have drained and contain ice for much of the year. Coal black in places, the lava is rusty red in others, and often dangerously sharp.

Pioneers who traveled through the area in the mid 1890s avoided this treacherous landscape, but hardy plants and animals make Craters of the Moon home. Along the Devils Orchard trail, modern explorers can spot small purple monkey flowers and rubber rabbitbrush. Dwarf mistletoe grows on limber pine, while pikas and marmots scurry into rock crevices. Each June, cinder-cone slopes sprout thousands of multicolored wildflowers. Flashlights and drinking water are *de rigueur* for foot travel and exploring the caves in Craters of the Moon.

Sawtooth Mountains and Sun Valley

Idaho Highway 75, the Sawtooth Scenic Route, climbs north from Ketchum toward the Sawtooth National Recreation Area. At Galena Summit, the long stretch of the Sawtooth Valley lies spread out beneath jagged granite peaks. Foothills—ancient glacial deposits covered with lodgepole pine—rim the valley. From these mountains springs the Salmon River. The Salmon flows northeast in this valley but will turn west to become the spectacular whitewater "River of No Return" farther north in Idaho. Three species of oceangoing salmon and steelhead travel over 800 miles from the Pacific Ocean to the upper Salmon River to spawn each year, a

Above: Rusty red remains of volcanic activity, Craters of the Moon National Monument.
GLENN VAN NIMWEGEN

Top, left: A hardy limber pine clings to pahoehoe *lava, Craters of the Moon.*
GLENN VAN NIMWEGEN

Left: Ski slopes and sheepherder's wagon and flock illustrate contrasts between old and new, Idaho.
JACK WILLIAMS

fisherman's dream during open season (obtain license and regulations locally).

Early natives harvested the wild root crop, camas lily. They fished for salmon and quarried local basalts for making stone arrowheads, scrapers, and knives. Later, pioneer explorers named the Sawtooth Range for its jagged profile. During the 1930s, railroad executive Averell Harriman enlisted the help of an Austrian count to find a territory in the west "of the same character as the Swiss and Austrian Alps," so he might build a resort—preferably, a site accessible only by his railroad. Soon after, construction began on Sun Valley ski resort. Sun Valley Lodge dates from 1936.

Writer Ernest Hemingway, a devotee of fishing, hunting, and the outdoors, spent the last years of his life here and was buried in the Ketchum cemetery in 1961. An Ernest Hemingway Memorial lies just northeast of Sun Valley Golf Course.

Because the Sawtooth Range borders no major highway, and there are no national parks close enough to bring in casual tourism, the range is one truly uncrowded summer recreation area. Wintertime is another story. The Rockies' original downhill ski resort, Sun Valley, still draws elite and moneyed crowds. The resort offers a staggering variety of organized or casual activities, depending on the season: ice skating, golf, tennis, running, bicycle riding, fishing, and horseback riding. Unusually stable updrafts give glider pilots a boost, and a chance to soar the Rockies.

The Surviving Wilderness

CHAPTER FOUR

Continuing up through vast, sparsely populated Wyoming, the state's north half is a land of frontier towns . . . and two of the West's most famous national parks.

Jackson Hole

A valley ringed by high mountains was called a "hole" by trappers and mountain men of the 1700s and early 1800s. This one was named for trapper David Jackson, and the "Jackson's Hole" area became a commercial center for the fur-trading business. Blackfeet, Crow, Flathead, Gros Ventre, Nez Perce, Bannock, and Shoshone Indians had all gathered plants and hunted in Jackson Hole, generally regarding it as neutral ground since winter weather made it too hostile for year-round tribal habitation.

As the nineteenth century passed and the twentieth rolled along, Jackson Hole developed as a base from which to see the Tetons. Summer and winter, an aerial tram climbs Rendezvous Mountain to a 10,450-foot lookout over contemporary Jackson Hole. The downhill ski area boasts a 4,139 foot vertical descent. July and August bring Jackson the annual Grand Teton Music Festival, increasingly famous among classical music circles.

Grand Teton National Park

Indians called the peaks *teewinot,* "many pinnacles," but lonely French trappers called the central peaks "Les Trois Tetons," the Three Breasts. A skyline found nowhere else, the Teton range rises precipitously out of Jackson Hole and the Idaho-side plains. Grand Teton's summit

Above: Western storefronts in downtown Jackson, Wyoming.
JACK WILLIAMS

Opposite: Glowing fall aspens and the Grand Teton, reflected in the Snake River.
LARRY ULRICH

Top: Winter willows, Grand Teton National Park.
GLENN VAN NIMWEGEN

*Top: Delicate pond
lilies and the
Grand Tetons.*
GLENN VAN NIMWEGEN

*Right: A sage grouse
cock displays his
mating plumage.*
DIANA STRATTON

*Far Right: Willow
twigs make a beaver's
winter meal.*
DIANA STRATTON

spears the clouds at 13,770 feet. Classic fault-block mountains, the Tetons formed when a 40-mile-long block of the earth's crust fractured and uplifted.

Extremely young on the geologic time scale, these mountains date back only about nine million years. As the Tetons rose in a series of earthquake-producing jolts, geologists estimate that a fault or break of ten feet or more occurred every few thousand years.

Alongside the upthrust Tetons, a second fault block—just as long and six to twelve miles wide—hinged downward at the same time to form the valley called Jackson Hole. This valley is estimated to have dropped four times more than the mountain block uplifted. The 40-mile fault separating the Teton block from Jackson Hole runs along the base of the Teton Range. Evidence for faulting includes the absence of foothills and the Tetons' extremely abrupt eastern front.

During three periods of global cooling, glacial ice carved the mountain range and filled in Jackson Hole. Thousands of feet of rocky material, later covered by a mile-deep deposit of white volcanic ash, were transported by glaciers to fill and re-level the down-dropping valley. Meltwater from glaciers and snowfalls enabled the Snake River to cut several terraces into thick deposits of cobbles and gravel left by earlier glaciers. Teton and Falling Ice Glaciers are two of twelve small remnants or re-entrants of the ice age that ended about 12,000 years ago.

Glacial moraines, long piles of rubble left behind when the glaciers receded, are visible inside the valley. Where meltwater has washed moisture-retaining clay and other materials out of stony glacial debris, only sagebrush, a few wildflowers, and grasses can grow. Alert observers may spot pronghorn antelope, coyote, and bison. On other ridges, dense stands of lodgepole pine offer concealment to elk, mule deer, black bear, red squirrels, and snowshoe hares.

In glacially carved canyons throughout the Teton range, aspen and evergreen forests rim meadows that fill in summer with yellow, red, white, and purple wildflowers. A superb challenge for mountaineers, the Tetons can be scaled via challenging beginner routes or expert alpinist's ascents. Unlike many mountain ranges, which require backpacking to reach even their foothill base camps, the Tetons are extremely accessible. Many of these peaks require only one day to climb—and a permit from Jenny Lake Ranger Station. Climbing instruction and guide service are also available. Ambitious and hardy visitors may even try ice climbing along white-knuckle-difficult routes.

Jenny Lake, a sapphire at the Tetons' feet, was named for the Shoshone Indian wife of trapper and guide Beaver Dick Leigh. Leigh guided an 1872 surveying expedition around Jackson Hole.

A winter view of the Snake River and Grand Tetons.
LEWIS KEMPER

Jenny Lake Lodge, site of a frontier homestead, operates as a guest ranch. The Lodge offers its guests fine dining in a classically rustic setting.

A mountainous portion of Grand Teton was designated as National Park in 1929, with the valley floor added in 1950, much to the credit of philanthropist/businessman John D. Rockefeller. Awed by the skyline and wildlife during a 1926 visit, Rockefeller began buying up land in Jackson Hole. In 1949 he deeded over 32,000 acres to the federal government.

Scenic roads wind through many wildlife habitats in Grand Teton National Park. Jenny Lake Scenic Loop is one of the most popular, but others include Signal Mountain Road (a five-mile, 800-foot climb to a vista encompassing the entire 40-mile Teton range) and the Willow Flats turnout (wet meadows and willow thickets where moose come to browse).

The Snake River runs a fairly smooth course through Jackson Hole, punctuated by rapids that are as challenging as most recreational paddlers might ever hope to float. Rafters spot moose and elk, small mammals, and birds along the shore.

Yellowstone National Park

Yellowstone is a land of change, where the earth's crust still rises, and ecosystems succeed one another in plain sight. A subcrustal "hot spot" like one underlying the Hawaiian island chain is believed to cause Yellowstone's unique thermal activity. About 600,000 years ago, the last of three catastrophic volcanic blasts spewed out nearly 240 cubic miles of debris and created the Yellowstone Caldera, a 28- by 47-mile basin (by comparison, Mount St. Helens' 1980 eruption blew out roughly a quarter of a cubic mile). Magmatic heat still runs the park's thermal theater of 10,000 geysers, hot springs, fumaroles, and mud pots.

Geysers require a powerful heat source (usually volcanic), plentiful water, and constrictions in the plumbing that prevent pressure from being vented steadily and continuously. Surface water seeps down into porous rock to be heated under pressure by magma from below. If the pressure drops, or water temperature rises high enough to overcome the pressure at depth, steam expands rapidly, forcing water out through the constriction. Hot springs bubble away without spectacular eruptions. Fumaroles vent steam. Mud pots form over acid-gas fumaroles that decompose rocks into mud and clay.

One thermal area where change is evident is Biscuit Basin, along the road from Madison Junction to Old Faithful. Mineral deposits took on 50-100 pound biscuit shapes, but a 1959 earthquake brought placid Sapphire Pool to life in a series of powerful eruptions. The resultant outflow tore loose the biscuits and washed nearly all of them away.

Old Faithful, Yellowstone's most famous geyser, existed as a hot spring for about 750 years, and began to erupt as a geyser perhaps 300 years ago. According to popular myth, its eruptions average a one-hour schedule. Actual intervals range from roughly 30 minutes to as long as 120 minutes. In the Old Faithful area, trails lead to a number of other notable thermal features including Emerald and Morning Glory Pools.

Norris Geyser Basin's unparalleled battery of thermal features—hottest in the park—includes unpredictable Steamboat Geyser, the world's largest. Steamboat has been known to hurl rocks 300-400 feet into the air, or to vent steam thousands of feet skyward.

At Mammoth Hot Springs, which has been called "a limestone cave turned inside out," water-deposited calcium carbonate forms spectacular, stairstep travertine terraces—including Minerva Terrace. Millions of algae live in the hot and warm terrace pools. The preference of different colored species for different water temperatures creates shades of brown, red, orange, and green in the pools. These springs and terraces change constantly: existing formations dry up or become more active, new springs appear, and old, inactive springs return to life.

In the Grand Canyon of the Yellowstone River, Upper and Lower Yellowstone Falls highlight the boundaries of ancient lava flows and thermal areas. All of the canyon colors—yellows, golds, pinks, and reds—are the result of hot water acting on volcanic rock; but Yellowstone Park is not named for this rock formation. The Yellowstone River joins the Missouri many miles downstream, outside National Park boundaries. There, Minnetaree Indians gave the waterway a name French trappers translated as *rouche jaune* or yellow stone.

Tower Fall, another spectacular cataract near Tower Junction along the Yellowstone loop road, is aptly named for nearby volcanic pinnacles. An easy path leads to Tower Fall's viewpoint, and there's a steep but rewarding walk to the base of the waterfall.

Yellowstone Lake occupies a glacially scoured portion of the Yellowstone Caldera. Lying close to the continental divide, Yellowstone Lake once drained toward the Pacific Ocean. As the watershed tilted, its outlet changed, draining it toward the Arctic Ocean by way of Hudson Bay. Now, Yellowstone Lake water travels to the Atlantic via the Gulf of Mexico. Just north of the lake, the Earth's surface is bulging roughly an inch a year, suggesting that magma beneath the park is rising today. The lake's West Thumb occupies a smaller, more recent caldera where lake sediments are heated from below.

Equally interesting is small Isa Lake, which drains to both the Atlantic Ocean (unexpectedly westward, through the Firehole, Madison, Missouri, and Mississippi Rivers) and eastward to the Pacific, by way of the Lewis, the Snake, and the Columbia.

More than sixty species of mammals, over 200 species of birds, and half a dozen game fish call Yellowstone home. Early morning and late evening, when animals come down along the rivers to drink and to graze, provide prime-time photography in several areas of Yellowstone National Park. Moose and bison often roam the Hayden Valley between Fishing Bridge and Canyon. Good viewing for elk, bison, and coyotes is in the Lamar Valley between Tower Junction and the Northeast Entrance. Pronghorn antelope often graze the sagebrush flats near Mammoth's north entrance, and bighorn sheep frequent Mount Washburn . . . but all of these ranges vary with the seasons. For current information, ask at a visitor center.

Other mammals to watch for include blacktail and whitetail deer, coyotes (Yellowstone's most common predator), elusive black bears and the even more secretive grizzly, lynx, and the rare mountain lion. Birds include trumpeter swans, pelicans, bald eagles, osprey, and Canada geese.

A black bear forages along the Gardiner River.
DIANA STRATTON

Yellowstone also has plenty of rodents, including two species of ground squirrels and three different chipmunks.

The National Parks and wildlands of the Rockies are home to North American animals in their natural environments . . . but Yellowstone is not a zoo. Animals live or die based on their ability to survive in this environment. Every year, incautious tourists are killed or maimed after approaching wild creatures too closely. Regulations separating humans from the wildlife protect *both*.

To give an example: Over several decades, Yellowstone bears came to depend on human food and garbage as easy substitutes for their more hard-won natural diet. Bears learned to associate people with food. The result was a situation that often brought bears into conflict with humans. New bear management practices that make garbage unavailable to bears mean fewer bear sightings but a more natural way of life

Above: Lower Falls from Artist Point, Grand Canyon of the Yellowstone.
LARRY ULRICH

Left: Early morning at Minerva Spring Terrace, Mammoth Hot Springs.
JEFF GNASS

Smoky light from the fires of 1988 lend a mysterious aspect to Clepsydra Geyser, Lower Geyser Basin, Yellowstone National Park.
LARRY ULRICH

for the protected black bears and grizzlies—and a safer environment for Park visitors.

The hardy lodgepole pine is Yellowstone's predominant evergreen. Some lodgepole cones are "serotinous," glued shut by pitch. The seeds are most readily released under intense heat of the kind that occurred during the 1988 summer of fires. Biologists estimate that naturally caused fires of this magnitude have blown through Yellowstone 300 times since vegetation re-appeared after the glaciers retreated 12,000 years ago. Drought and high winds sparked the climax of Yellowstone's natural fire cycle for the first time in recorded history.

Fires burned in a "mosaic" pattern. Sparks flew on the wind from one zone to another, often leaving large areas virtually untouched. Near Gibbon Meadows, an excellent example of "mosaic" burn is visible along the highway. Like people, forests change. Slowly, lodgepole seed-

lings—the first tree species to establish after a fire—are reclaiming the burned areas.

Many tribes of Indians hunted and fished inside the boundaries of Yellowstone National Park. Black volcanic glass, quarried at Obsidian Cliff (on the Park's west side between Norris and Mammoth Hot Springs), was fashioned into cutting implements and projectile points by native toolmakers, and traded across North America. A roadside marker along the highway from Madison Junction to Old Faithful commemorates the flight of Chief Joseph and the Nez Perce Indians through the river valleys of Yellowstone.

John Colter of the Lewis and Clark expedition may have been the first non-Indian to visit the Yellowstone area, in 1806. Wounded in a battle between Crow and Blackfeet Indians on his way back to civilization, he carried out tales of fire and brimstone. Listeners dismissed them as the result of wound-induced delirium.

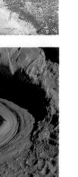

Above: Old Faithful, Yellowstone's most famous geyser.
JEFF GNASS

Left: A walkway leads visitors past many-hued Grand Prismatic Spring, Midway Geyser Basin.
LARRY ULRICH

Below: Bubbling mudpots, Pocket Basin, Yellowstone National Park.
JEFF GNASS

Jim Bridger passed through in 1857 and told similar stories. Geologist and explorer F.V. Hayden took Bridger seriously and initiated a reconnaissance interrupted by the Civil War. Definitive exploration of Yellowstone began in 1869, and in 1871 Hayden's scientific survey brought back evidence that finally convinced a disbelieving country.

President Ulysses S. Grant proclaimed Yellowstone the world's first national park in 1872, but Congress did not vote funds to administer it until 1918. The Headquarters town of Mammoth Hot Springs was the site of Fort Yellowstone, built during the era when U.S. Army troops administered Yellowstone Park.

Five entrances and a figure-eight road system provide access to Yellowstone National Park's major attractions. Northernmost roads remain open all winter from Yellowstone's North Entrance near Gardiner to Cooke City, Montana,

Changing colors along the Gardiner River, Yellowstone National Park.
SANDY NYKERK

but other Park roads close in October or November to reopen in April or May. During the winter season (mid-December to mid-March), non-automotive travel through Yellowstone is possible. Snowmobiles and snowcoaches (buses that motivate on tractor treads and skis) enter via the West, South, and East Entrances, and depart from a staging area in Mammoth Hot Springs. Cross-country skis provide another popular option.

Self-guiding trails offer on-the-spot geological and biological education in such areas as Mammoth Hot Springs Terraces, Fountain Paint Pots, Norris Geyser Basin, Mud Volcano, Old Faithful area, and Grand Canyon of the Yellowstone. A thousand miles of trails take hikers, horseback riders, and cross-country skiers into vast, primitive back country . . . and to rarely photographed geysers, fumaroles, and hot pools.

But there is plenty to see along Yellowstone's loop roads. The immense Yellowstone Caldera shows most plainly from the Washburn Hot Springs Overlook south of Dunraven Pass. For varying degrees of 1988 fire damage, the most spectacular Park approach is between West Yellowstone and Madison Junction. Even the burned tracts spark their own kind of awe for the slow-rung changes of natural succession.

Historic accommodations include Mammoth Hot Springs Hotel, rustic Roosevelt Lodge, and elegant Lake Yellowstone Hotel. At Old Faithful, the historic wooden Inn was saved by heroic firefighting efforts from a 1988 firestorm, as were contemporary Old Faithful Snow Lodge (open summer and winter) and the Old Faithful Lodge.

Wintry weather is possible at any time in Yellowstone National Park—the lowest recorded summer temperature was 9 degrees in August 1910, at the Canyon weather station—so it's wise to call or write ahead for weather information.

Cody and Buffalo Bill Country

Where the Rockies meet the great American plains, the town of Cody lies east of Yellowstone Park on Wyoming Highways 14, 16, and 20. This combined route follows the North Fork of the Shoshone River through the Wapiti Valley, named after an Indian word for elk. It's no surprise to find elk grazing along the Shoshone. Between Yellowstone's East Entrance and Cody, travelers can take advantage of numerous lodges, outfitters, and guest ranches.

Buffalo Bill Cody earned his nickname by supplying railroad workers with meat. One of the most illustrious prairie scouts of the Indian wars, he received the Congressional Medal of Honor in 1872. In partnership with an irrigation company, Cody founded the frontier town that bears his name in 1895—a few tent and frame buildings.

Cody built the Irma Hotel (named for his daughter) to accommodate wayfarers who rode the railroad in. Filled with Victorian furnishings and Western memorabilia, the Irma remains a Cody landmark.

Trout fishing, rodeo, golf, and whitewater or scenic flatwater raft trips attract travelers to Cody, but its prime drawing card is the Buffalo Bill Historical Center, four museums in a single complex. Memorabilia from the career of city founder Buffalo Bill, from saddles to trophies, fill one museum. Another museum portrays the history of Plains Indian tribes. Near at hand, alongside early American matchlocks and flint-locks, lies the final repository for the entire collection of Winchester rifles, shotguns, and Army weapons. Artwork by Remington, Russell, Catlin, Moran, and other Western masters fills

Above: Serene Trout Creek, in Yellowstone's Hayden Valley.
LARRY ULRICH

Left: Alpine wildflowers carpet the Beartooth Plateau, Shoshone National Forest, Wyoming.
JEFF GNASS

37

Above: Flyfishing in the Green River, Bridger National Forest, Wyoming.
LARRY ULRICH

Right: Bull elk, Montana.
RICK MC INTYRE

the Whitney Gallery of Western Art, with seasonal exhibits that change twice yearly. An annual Plains Indian Powwow every June brings representatives from the tribes to participate in dance competitions and reenact ancient rituals in an outdoor amphitheater on museum grounds.

Another Cody attraction is Old Trail Town, where two dozen historic buildings stand (including one used by Butch Cassidy and his Hole in the Wall Gang), restored and relocated from numerous Wyoming locations.

From Cody, a memorable loop northwest along Wyoming 120, U.S. 212, and Wyoming 296 crosses Beartooth Pass, a U.S. Forest Service National Scenic Byway comparable to Rocky Mountain National Park's Trail Ridge Road or Glacier's Going-to-the-Sun Road. The Beartooth Highway traverses a glacier-carved plateau high above treeline and dotted with tiny lakes. Returning to Cody, a side trip on the gravel road to Sunlight Basin offers glimpses of pastoral ranch country.

Devils Tower National Monument

Almost the width of Wyoming—300 miles—separates Devils Tower National Monument from Yellowstone and the Rockies, but from Cody that's barely a skip by western standards. This eroded trachyte plug of an ancient volcano stands alone on the plains in view of South Dakota's Black Hills. Devils Tower rises 1,280 feet from the valley floor to a summit 5,117 feet above sea level. President Theodore Roosevelt, an ardent conservationist, proclaimed Devils Tower the first U.S. National Monument in 1906.

Kiowa Indians explained the Tower's deeply grooved columnar sides as the scratches left by a giant bear attempting to claw its way to the top. Mateo Tepee or "bear lodge" was the most common Indian name for the tower. Native Americans were guaranteed possession of all the land in this area as the Great Sioux Reservation by the Fort Laramie Treaty of 1868. But once General George Armstrong Custer confirmed the presence of gold in the Black Hills, treaties counted for nothing. Settlers and the Army drove the Indians out, and pioneers came to pasture cattle on spacious grasslands around the landmark surveyors dubbed "Devil's Tower."

For ranchers in the late 1800s, isolated by miles from one another, Devils Tower became a Fourth-of-July meeting place. The first "official" climb was made on July 4, 1893, by the flag-carrying team of William Rogers and Willard Ripley . . . but conveniently, a flagpole already perched atop the Tower (planted, it is suspected, by Rogers and Ripley in advance of their official ascent). Early climbers used a wooden stake ladder. In 1937, Fritz Wiessner, the father of technical rock climbing in the U.S., was the first to ascend Devils Tower using technical means. In 1938, Jack Durrance pioneered a route still considered the easiest on the Tower. Eventually, over 100 climbing routes of varying difficulty were pioneered. Jan and Herb Conn, Tower climbers in the 1940s and 1950s, later moved underground in the nearby Black Hills to map and explore Jewel Cave National Monument. Because of their efforts, Jewel Cave is acknowledged as one of the world's longest explored caverns.

Mountains and plains converge at Devils Tower, providing habitat for more than 90 species of birds, including hawks, eagles, and the prairie falcon. There are also rattlesnakes, so visitors should explore cautiously.

A one-mile trail circumnavigates the Tower's base through the rubble of fallen trachyte columns. All climbers who wish to ascend the Tower must register with a Park ranger. Depending on a climber's expertise, physical condition, and chosen route, the ascent may take an hour or the better part of a day.

Incredibly, wildlife survives up on the top. Grasses, sagebrush, currant bushes, and prickly pear cacti have been photographed atop Devils Tower, as well as rattlesnakes, chipmunks, and birds.

Above: An alert prairie dog, Devils Tower National Monument.
SANDY NYKERK

Below: 1,280-foot Devils Tower, in eastern Wyoming.
GLENN VAN NIMWEGEN

39

Under Western Skies

I s the big sky state's sky really any larger? Perhaps not, but from a Montana vantage high on the north end of the U.S. continental divide, that sky seems as limitless as the western prairies. Formerly crossed by natives and emigrants—who left several historic sites in the Rocky Mountains' shadow—the grassy prairies now ripple with "amber waves of grain."

Custer Battlefield National Monument

Returning from Devils Tower along Interstate 90 toward southern Montana's Rockies, it's possible to stroll the spot where George Armstrong Custer's career ended at the Battle of the Little Big Horn. Between Crow Agency and Garryowen, two small towns on the Crow Indian Reservation, Custer Battlefield National Monument is peaceful now, and prairie grasses nod quietly in the wind.

Custer's "last stand" took place on June 25, 1876, when General Custer and about 210 men of his force were killed by Sioux and Northern Cheyenne Indians. Just south of the National Monument, Reno-Benteen Battlefield Memorial honors two (perhaps less impetuous) commanders who survived a second battle nearby. Reno's men had the chore of burying Custer's command. Indians who fell were carried away by their comrades; some Native American survivors later joined Buffalo Bill's Wild West Show.

Bighorn Canyon National Recreation Area

South of the Crow Reservation, the Bighorn River has cut a magnificent canyon deep into

Above: American Bison in grassland habitat, Moiese National Bison Range, Montana.
CAROL HAVENS

Opposite: A hiker's view of Gunsight Pass, Glacier National Park, Montana.
DAN TYERS

Top: A profusion of Rockies wildflowers.
GLENN VAN NIMWEGEN

Above: Markers on grassy slopes commemorate the 1876 Battle of the Little Big Horn, Custer Battlefield National Monument.
SANDY NYKERK

Right: The Bighorn River flows between towering rock walls, Bighorn Canyon National Recreation Area.
JEFF GNASS

pastel-tinted sedimentary rock. Nearby is the National Wild Horse and Wildlife Range, home of a large herd of mingled Spanish- and Anglo-released mustangs. Vast Bighorn Lake backs up behind the Yellowtail Dam, bordered by rock walls towering hundreds of feet over the shore.

Museum of the Rockies

"One place through all of time," the Museum of the Rockies straddles a low hill on the edge of Bozeman near Montana State University. Juxtaposing ancient and modern, past and future, the contents of the museum's collections range in age from prehistoric relics to mid-twentieth century. The Museum also boasts the high-technology Taylor Planetarium, a family of life-sized animated triceratops, and contemporary Western art.

Perhaps its most fascinating display room presents aspects of dinosaur life that have only recently been suggested. A life-sized model maiasaur ("good mother lizard") feeds her young in a bowl-shaped earthen nest, surrounded by plants and animals that shared the dinosaurs' ancient world. A growing collection of dinosaur remains, all found in Montana, includes clutches of fossilized *Maiasaurus peeblesorum* eggs still embedded in gray parent rock and one of the most complete *Tyrannosaurus rex* skeletons ever found.

Virginia City and Nevada City

Countless mining towns sprang up over gold veins in the Rockies during the 1800s. At Virginia City, the strikes were better than many. During the height of the Montana gold rush about mid-century, outlaws operating in cahoots with Sheriff Plummer and his dubious law enforcement gang got the upper hand on justice until citizens organized a vigilante committee that hanged thirty-two road agents in four months.

Continuously settled since gold rush days, much of Virginia City's Main Street was restored during the 1950s and 1960s in an effort spearheaded by Charlie Bovey and his family. Tourists can load up a sack with old-time candies at one end of town and stroll the boardwalk to the other end for an 1890s-style musical revue and melodrama. A narrow-gauge railroad ride (or Montana highway 287) leads to nearby Nevada City, an entire town restored as an open air museum. Realistic "road agents" hold up conductors along the narrow-gauge line in summer months. Drop a quarter and run for your life in the music hall, where coin-operated banks of organs, violins, horns, pianos, and drums entertain as loudly as when they were built . . . even if they have gone slightly out of tune.

Western Montana Forests and Mountains

As the Rockies' crest winds north through Montana, it passes through the Beaverhead, Gallatin, Deerlodge, Lolo, Helena, Lewis & Clark, Flathead, and Kootenai National Forests. Hundreds of lakes and rivers make the western quarter of Montana a virtually continuous recreation area.

Montana's first pioneers came hoping to find gold, but timber, cattle, and tourism now head the region's list of income sources. Winter temperatures may plunge well below zero. The dry, fluffy

snow of the Montana Rockies lures alpine and nordic skiers, snowmobilers, and travelers eager for quiet, cool solitude. Many resorts remain open almost the year around, including the Lone Mountain Guest Ranch at Big Sky, which converts operations from summer horse-and-flyfishing guest ranching into a gourmet paradise for nordic skiers.

The city of Butte lies atop "the richest hill on Earth" in west-central Montana, where copper, silver, and other precious metals have been scratched out of enormous pit mines. Butte's Irish-extracted citizens conduct Saint Patrick's Day festivities that rival New York's for enthusiasm and community participation.

South of Glacier National Park, the Bob Marshall Wilderness honors hiker and forester Marshall, who helped found the Wilderness Society in 1935 and was named head of the U.S. Division of Recreation and Lands in 1937. The Bob Marshall Wilderness surrounds Sphinx Peak, Silvertip Mountain, and other giants of the continental divide. Here is true wilderness, where grizzlies outnumber hikers and the promise of adventure is very, very real.

Above, left: A window into the boom town past of Virginia City, Montana.
SANDY NYKERK

Above: Sunset over Lone Mountain, the Gallatin Range, near Big Sky, Montana.
TOM NELSON

Glacier National Park

Since 1818, the 49th parallel has formed the boundary between the western United States and Canada. In Waterton-Glacier International Peace Park, that boundary is marked only by a swath of downed timber. Hikers may cross it as freely as the eagles fly over it.

A fault block 300 miles long slowly slid forty miles eastward in the Glacier Park region about 65 million years ago. These strong rocks moved like a massive sheet propelled over soft shales, creating the great Lewis Overthrust.

From that fault block, Pleistocene glaciers carved the ridges and pinnacles of Glacier National Park. Hanging valleys, where small side glaciers joined deeper and larger ones, now drop ethereal waterfalls to the U-shaped valleys' floors. Horn-shaped Mount Clements, Kinnerly Peak, and Mount Wilbur were glacially carved on three or even four sides. Mid-park, jagged Ptarmigan Wall is about 4.5 miles long, thousands of feet tall from either valley floor, and so narrow in places that a climber can hang a leg over each side.

The Park's active glaciers, found between elevations of 6000 and 9000 feet, are shrinking. Grinnell Glacier, now about 275 acres, was twice that large a hundred years ago. Precipitation has dropped and the climate has warmed since these glaciers reached their maximum extent several thousand years ago. No one is certain how much the process has been hastened by the atmospheric buildup of carbon dioxide and other "greenhouse" gases.

Glacier National Park's topography is markedly different from that of regions farther south. These angled, banded slopes and summits are made up of layered sedimentary and lightly metamorphosed rocks, not the granitic and intensely metamorphosed rocks of Rocky Mountain National Park. Easy to observe high along the Garden Wall, Mount Wilbur, and other peaks, is a clearly visible diorite sill: a horizontal dark band between layers of light-colored rock. This diorite sill formed when very hot magma flowed up into limestone beds. The sill and its heat-bleached enclosing beds are easily traced all over the park. Triple Divide Peak, unique in the United States, sheds water west toward the Pacific, northeast toward Hudson Bay, and southeast toward the Gulf of Mexico.

Glacier's wide range of climates and altitudes provides niches for diverse flora and fauna. Western slopes, where more precipitation falls, support dark, thick forests of spruce, fir, cedar, larch, and pine with dense undergrowth. On windswept eastern slopes grow species requiring less moisture: spruce and subalpine fir, aspen and prairie grasses.

Midsummer hikers share huckleberries, raspberries, thimbleberries, and wild strawberries with black bears and grizzlies. The official Park

Clouds nestle among peaks of the Continental Divide near Logan Pass, Glacier National Park.
RICK MC INTYRE

Service warning reads, "Be aware in bear country! For your safety talk to a ranger before hiking." High in alpine meadows reached only by the Park's 730 miles of beautifully planned and maintained backcountry trails—and by one spectacular road—grow beargrass and glacier lily, heather, and gentian and a dazzling array of other wildflowers.

Glacier National Park's human history dates back as far as any in North America. According to Piegan Indian legend, the Old North Trail (still faintly visible in the vicinity of East Glacier) "originated with the migration of a 'great tribe' of

Indians from the distant north to the south"—possibly the first movement of Asian peoples into the plains country of North America. During the Mountain Man era, this area belonged to the Blackfeet Indian Nation, and Blackfeet still consider Glacier Park lands to be sacred ground.

Going-to-the-Sun Road is named after a nearby mountain. According to a variant of one Blackfeet legend, the god Napi helped his people in a time of trouble, then returned to his home in the sun from this mountaintop. The road was completed in 1933; however, each spring it must be reopened, dug out from beneath forty-foot

Above: Glacially carved peaks tower over Wild Goose Island on Saint Mary Lake, Glacier National Park.
LARRY ULRICH

Left: Black bear cub.
DIANA STRATTON

45

Glacier National Park's Going-to-the-Sun Road, completed in 1933, crosses the Continental Divide with breathtaking views of Rockies peaks, waterfalls, and glaciers.
JEFF GNASS

snowdrifts that linger into June. An engineering marvel that took private and governmental crews fourteen years to build at a cost of three million dollars, the 50-mile trip across the continental divide redefines the word "breathtaking," traversing vertical cliffs, climbing the mountainside to Logan Pass, then plunging into a glacial valley on the other side. The contrasting climates of east and west slopes balance one another on two sides of an alpine pass through meadows so fragile every footstep leaves a scar. Logan Pass Visitor

Center offers interpretive displays on the alpine environment. Because Going-to-the-Sun Road was constructed for small 1930s cars, rangers enforce vehicle length limits during peak season.

Glacier National Park was established in 1910. Four of the Park's eight lodges, built to draw railroad travelers, date back to that decade. Each hotel has its own motif. Lake McDonald Lodge is built in the style of an early hunting retreat.

Steeped in Swiss-Alps ambience, Many Glacier Hotel lies near the end of a spur road from Babb,

*Above: A sure-footed
mountain goat.*
RICK MC INTYRE

*Left: Mt. Wilbur
looms over slopes
carpeted in beargrass,
Many Glacier area.*
GLENN VAN NIMWEGEN

*Below: Summer
wildflowers at Glacier
National Park's
Logan Pass include
Indian paintbrush and
Lewis's monkeyflower.*
LARRY ULRICH

Montana, and is often considered the heart of
Glacier National Park. Mount Wilbur, Mount
Gould, and Grinnell Point tower like gray giants
over windy Swiftcurrent and Josephine Lakes,
with the Garden and Pinnacle Walls looming
behind them. From this hub, trails lead off into
rugged scenery that surrounds the tiny settle-
ment. Bighorn sheep frequent the area. At Many
Glacier and other locations, wranglers operate
horseback-riding concessions, and Many Glacier
employees traditionally present first-class nightly
musical entertainment.

Sperry and Granite Park Chalets, backcountry hotels accessible only by trail, were built
in 1914 out of native stone. Both are on the
National Register of Historic Places. Accommodations are primitive but warm, and three meals
included in the price of a night's lodging supply
energy for the hike back out.

Raft companies offer day trips on the North
and Middle Forks of the Flathead River, which
border the Park. Canoes and rowboats may be
used on most lakes inside Glacier's boundaries,
and regulations allow motorboats on some.
Concession employees pilot excursion boat
cruises on six of the largest lakes. Many streams
and lakes are open for fishing.

Wildflowers at Logan Pass,
Glacier National Park.
LARRY ULRICH
Opposite: The skyline of
Mt. Heavens, Glacier National Park.
LEWIS KEMPER